MORE
SIMPLY
PILATES

HINKLER
BOOKS

Assistant Coordinator: Rodney Searle
Art Director: Karen Moores
Graphic Artist: Susie Allen
Photographer: Glenn Weiss

First published in 2004 by Hinkler Books Pty Ltd
17-23 Redwood Drive
Dingley, VIC 3172 Australia
www.hinklerbooks.com

Printed and bound in China

First printed in 2005

ISBN 1 7412 1796 2

CONTENTS

INTRODUCTION

Pilates is often described as the 'intelligent workout' as it is a movement-based discipline that also aligns itself with the 'less is more' exercise principle.

Although the Pilates Method was developed almost a century ago, recognition of its many benefits has grown during recent years. In the early 1900s, German-born Joseph Pilates devised a system of movement, undertaken in a particular sequence, that would achieve and maintain an individual's optimal level of overall mind/body fitness. The basis of his philosophy came from his knowledge of various exercise principles. Following his death in the 1960s, Joseph's legacy was continued initially by his students, and has evolved over the years into various and similar forms, though the principles remain the same.

People from all walks of life have gained benefit from the Method. Dancers and celebrities have long been known to incorporate Pilates into their lifestyle schedule. This continuing trend amongst the rich, famous and beautiful has led to recent mainstream popularity of the Method.

While a strong, toned and elongated body is frequently the sought after reward for many fitness conscious individuals, any aesthetic value in muscle development is actually a secondary bonus to the functional musculo-skeletal benefits gained from a sensible and committed approach to the Pilates Method.

When practised as it was intended – as a postural retraining method, both generally and through movement – Pilates exercises help restore symmetry to the body, thus aiding in the development of, or restoring of, balanced strength up to any level attainable.

The Pilates Method is a system of movement-based mind-body conditioning exercises. It is suitable for everyone from people with general and rehabilitative needs through to the elite athlete, providing the individual applies their concentration and imagination! As strengthening the muscles supports the joints, a growing number of physical practitioners regard the Pilates Method as an appropriate complement to the treatment and prevention of injury.

'Less is more' with sensible exercising, so restrict the number of repetitions of each exercise – in accordance with your ability – to maintain correct form. If you experience joint pain, seek advice from a qualified professional rather than pushing through the pain barrier!

BENEFITS

A regular 'mind-body conditioning routine' should be considered a wise investment in the future of our health. As we age, our bodies succumb to natural degenerative changes. However, choosing to incorporate a 'holistic approach' to exercising will maintain your optimal mobility and agility.

Pilates mat work re-educates an individual how to best place, move and coordinate their body. Like any worthwhile endeavour, this is obviously a process that's difficult to improve upon, if there is no real commitment to practice! Pilates is a 'way' of exercising as much as it is a sequence of exercises...and the benefits are many and effective, regardless of age or fitness level.

Pilates is all about restoring balance and symmetry throughout the body – ie, the stability and mobility of joints; and the suppleness and strength of muscles.

Furthermore, regular practise of the Pilates philosophy will promote relaxation, complete body control, movement articulation and coordination, as well as increased energy levels and a more confident posture.

The versatility of Pilates exercises for different fitness needs is also widely recognised. Greater confidence and coordination in movement execution for both functional (general, everyday movement) and specific/sophisticated means (such as sports) is certainly achievable.

More Simply Pilates will draw your attention to the benefits of moving the body in a methodical and articulate manner, allowing you to gain abdominal, back and hip strength in a way that is safe for your spine. You will experience greater control over movement and breathing, and your strength gained will give a true sense of stability with elongated muscle tone, rather than superficial muscle bulk. In addition, your posture will become more effortless from the strength and mobility exercises for your upper back and shoulders.

PILATES PRINCIPLES

The following fundamental points are based on Joseph Pilates' beliefs outlining how the movement is to be executed, in order to achieve the benefits it does. Pilates is 'pilates' because of the 'way' the exercises are articulately done. Integrating these principles into the way you move is exercising 'intelligently' for the longevity of your body.

- Concentration • Control • Centring
- Fluidity • Precision • Breathing

Because Pilates is very much a mind workout – requiring inward focus and concentration on a number of things at once – the movement is often taught by the use of 'images'. A vivid imagination is an advantage when learning the Pilates 'way' of body conditioning. Imagery is a powerful tool in assisting an individual to correctly execute and articulate the exercises. This helps facilitate a deeper, more kinesthetic awareness of musculoskeletal mechanics and movement dynamics. Visualisation also assists with breathing flow and/or dynamics. It is important to realise how Pilates is not about 'working hard' and 'burning' your muscles. That may come after you achieve the fundamentals! You want to train your mind first – body awareness is a must so that your journey with the Pilates Method can be one of 'discovering' how you can get your body to move with the greatest of ease.

PRACTICAL MATTERS

There are generally a set of standard Pilates mat exercises which are traditionally broken up into 'basic', 'intermediate' and 'advanced' levels of difficulty. It is important to realise your own physical capabilities when embarking on any new activity. Concentrate on the quality of your personal execution of an exercise sequence and not on the choreography of fancy movement. Pilates is a 'sensible approach' to correcting and maintaining postural alignment, strength and suppleness. Try to regard your practise of Pilates much like 'building blocks' – master your abilities step by step and don't execute movement sequences that may cause you to forego correct placement and stability.

Firstly read and acknowledge the information relating to correct abdominal bracing and body alignment and then proceed with the workout at a pace suitable to your fitness level.

In the case of injury, or physical limitations, seek advice from your physical practitioner prior to starting any new exercise program. Pilates is not recommended if you are pregnant unless you have previously been attending regular sessions and you have clearance from your doctor. Your qualified Pilates instructor may develop an appropriate workout program for you. Depending on what your physical life entails, two to four Pilates workouts a week is optimal, as it's the consistency that will ensure full benefit. Remember, the 'less is more' philosophy with sensible exercising.

Requirements

You will need certain accessories in order to do your Pilates mat workout. The mat or carpet surface must offer some comfort, but must not be so soft that your body sinks into it, as this causes your spine to lose the integrity of its natural curvature. In addition, you will need a small pillow and a towel to assist you with some exercises and stretches. (You may also use these to rest your head and neck upon for support.) Finally, it is recommended that you use a low chair or box to relieve lower back tension during some of the 'sitting' exercises.

CENTRING AND BREATHING

Always commence your Pilates workout quietly, focusing on some important concepts that will be your priority during the exercises so that you can maximise the benefits.

NEUTRAL PELVIS is a term that describes the position of the pelvis when the spine is in its natural position. Usually, your hip bones (iliac crests) and your pubic bone should form a parallel level with the floor. Your lower back should not be pressed into the floor, nor should it be over arched. This creates the best position for your deeper abdominal muscles to be strengthened.

BREATHING is important to focus on, but don't become consumed by the need to breathe too deeply or artificially just to do the exercises. Breathe normally, accenting the exhale, and try to develop a different way of breathing that will help you keep 'control' of your abdominal muscles. In Pilates we call this 'lateral breathing', which means to direct the breath into the side and back of the lower ribcage.

ABDOMINAL ACTIVATION in Pilates is a major priority. It is not about the sheer effort of contracting these muscles, but rather the subtleness of refining how you do so. Don't ever clench your muscles or allow the stomach to pop up. Draw the muscles of the pelvic floor up and gently press the lower abdominals to the spine.

Your deep abdominal muscles act like reinforcement for the joints of your spine. When you combine this action with regular breathing, make sure your neck is relaxed and your ribs don't protrude. Imagine a pin at the base of your ribs while you breathe laterally and simply scoop your lower abdominals inward and upward. With each exhale, imagine your waist shrinking.

CENTRING AND BREATHING

(continued)

PREPARATORY NOTE: The essence of Pilates starts with the placement of your pelvis, ribcage, scapulae (shoulder blades) and head – as movement or displacement of any, or all of these effects the curves of the spine. Once you are 'aligned' then turn your focus to the coordination of your breath and abdominal bracing action. The Method is all about maintaining a posture that is simple and natural; maintaining a natural breathing rhythm and learning how to facilitate gentle and effective abdominal bracing for lumbo-pelvic stability.

Movement on any level comes after this awareness of 'stabilising' the torso. Your limbs should be easily mobile without losing a strong sense of 'centre' – referred to now as 'core stability'. Joseph Pilates referred to the muscles around the 'centre' as the 'powerhouse'.

BREATHING EXERCISE

1 Lie on your back with your legs bent and heels in line with your sitting bones. (This position will be referred to as a 'preparatory' position, as all exercises that begin on your back must start in a neutral alignment.)

2 Rest your hands on your abdomen and draw your attention to how you are breathing. As you inhale visualise doing so through the back and sides of your lower ribcage so that your deep abdominal muscles can remain braced. Try not to elevate your shoulders or change the shape of your spine.

3 As you exhale, emphasise a deeper drawing in action of your lower abdominals. Try to imagine the front of your spine, especially where it joins the pelvis. Lift your pelvic floor muscles and scoop your deep lower abdominal muscles (like an 'inward-upward' action) in order to give you a sensation of stabilising the lower back.

Breathe normally and not too quickly so as to train yourself to do this in a way that is functional for everyday. Be careful not to allow your ribs to arch off the floor and be conscious to relax muscles you don't need to use (eg. your hips and thighs).

WARM UP

Purpose *The warm up enables you to establish and practise the basic principles of Pilates with simple movements. This is also preparing you for subsequent exercises.*

HIP MOBILITY

1 Start in your preparatory position. As you breathe in, open one knee to the side and slide the same foot directly away from your sitting bone. Straighten this leg and aim to keep both hips still on the floor and keep your other leg tension free. Do not arch your back.

2 Exhale, rotating your leg inward and drawing the heel back toward your sitting bone. Keep your ribcage fairly flat on the floor, your pelvis anchored and your abdominals flat and strong.

3 Repeat on the same side in the same direction. Do 3-4 repetitions of these in each direction, with each leg.

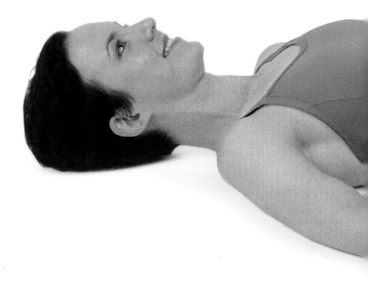

WARM UP

(continued)

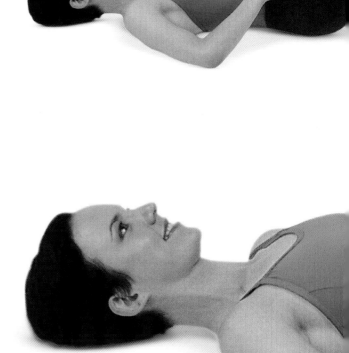

LEG FLOATS

1 Start in your preparatory position with your abdominal muscles braced. Inhale as you lift one knee toward you, keeping the shin bone parallel to the floor.

2 Exhale as you extend the leg away from you, only as far as you can keep your pelvis and ribcage still and symmetrical. Visualise shrinking through your waist and pulling your navel area to your spine.

3 Breathe in as you bend your leg back toward you, maintaining the lift of your pelvic floor and deep abdominals.

4 Exhale as you replace the foot to the floor.

5 Alternate legs for 6-10 repetitions.

NOTE
Remember not to focus too much on limb movement. The movement develops your coordination and challenges your trunk stability, while you gain abdominal strength and endurance in preparation for later exercises.

WARM UP

(continued)

SCAPULA MOVEMENT

1 Stay in your preparatory position and raise your arms toward the ceiling, slightly wider than shoulder width apart. Nod your chin gently and maintain a sense of stability around your waist.

2 As you inhale, reach your arms toward the ceiling to produce movement of the shoulder blades 'forward', while not affecting your neck position. Your shoulders should not elevate toward your head.

3 Breathe out (keep reaching your fingers up to create some resistance) as you retract your shoulders down toward the back of your waist, without moving your ribcage or head and neck.

4 Continue for 6-10 repetitions.

NOTE
This exercise will assist you in learning how to best stabilise your shoulder blades as they are required to sit flat against the back of your ribcage throughout many of the Pilates exercises. This strengthens your middle back muscles for better posture.

ARM CIRCLES

1 Begin as you did for Scapula Movement. Inhale as you take your arms overhead without moving your ribcage or shoulder blades.

2 As you exhale, face your palms toward the ceiling and draw your arms, in a wide circle, down to your sides. Keep your chest open so you don't become round shouldered and remember to maintain taut abdominals.

3 Repeat 3-5 times, then reverse the circles.

Warm Up

(continued)

Chest Lift

1 Stay in your preparatory alignment and place your hands behind your head, keeping both elbows within your vision. Draw your shoulder blades down, keeping your ribcage and pelvis anchored to the floor and shrink through your abdominal area. Inhale.

2 As you exhale, roll your chest forward, dropping your chin gently and pressing your lower ribcage down toward the floor. Keep your legs relaxed and your pelvis anchored on the floor.

3 Inhale, hold still and strong, being careful not to allow your ribs to release from the floor or your abdomen to 'pop' up. Visualise breathing into your back and keep your shoulders stable.

4 Roll down as you exhale, keep scooping your abdominals toward your spine so that you develop variations in strength.

5 Repeat 5-10 times.

> **NOTE**
> The Chest Lift is the basis of more advanced Pilates abdominal work and your priority is to address all the fundamental principles outlined so far.

DOUBLE LEG SLIDES

1 Maintain the preparatory position. Place your hands on your hip and waist region so that you will be aware if any unnecessary movement occurs. Breathe in, drawing your deep abdominals inward and upward like an internal zip.

2 As you exhale, slide both feet directly away from you, emphasising a slight pressing down of the abdomen and lower back toward the floor, so that you reinforce your spine.

3 Breathe in, maintaining your posture. Ensure that your shoulder blades are drawn down and your ribs stay on the floor.

4 Slide your heels back toward your sitting bones as you exhale. Visualise a connection between your shoulders drawing down, abdominals shrinking and your lower ribcage pressing into the floor.

5 Repeat 3-5 times before combining with the Chest Lift exercise.

Warm Up

(continued)

Double Leg Slides *(continued)*

6 Start as you would for Chest Lift. Inhale.

7 Exhale, roll forward, pressing your lower ribs toward the floor and shrink through your waist. Inhale, hold still.

8 Exhale as you slide your feet away – only as far as you can maintain your Chest Lift position. Don't allow your back or pelvis to move. Inhale, hold.

9 As you exhale draw your heels back toward you. Keep your shoulders drawing down and emphasise scooped in abdominals. Inhale, hold.

10 Exhale as you roll back down.

11 Repeat 3-5 times.

Note
Remember that your Warm Up exercises should be treated as the blueprint for more difficult exercises. Keep your pelvis and ribcage stable and your waist and shoulders strong. Start to elongate your exhales to facilitate a deeper sense of abdominal strength.

CHEST LIFT HOLDING

1 Begin as for the Chest Lift. Breathe in, preparing your abdominal muscles, careful not to arch your ribs off the floor.

2 As you exhale, roll your chest forward without moving your pelvis.

3 Maintain this position and continue breathing calmly. With each inhale, don't allow yourself to lie down at all and with each exhale, emphasise deeper abdominals and shoulders down. Relax your thighs and hips.

4 Continue breathing; count 5-6 inhales. Exhale, roll down.

WARM UP

(continued)

HUNDRED

1 Begin in your preparatory position. Lift one leg at a time to a 'tabletop' position. Feel that the back of your pelvis and ribcage are anchored on the floor, that your shoulders are relaxed and that your abdominals are zipped firmly. Assume a calm breathing pattern. Place your arms by your sides.

2 As you exhale, nod your chin down gently and roll your ribcage forward, reaching your arms alongside you just off the floor. Press your stomach deep toward your spine, stabilising your hip bones on the floor. Extend your legs only as far as your trunk is stable, or maintain the legs at tabletop.

3 Keep this position strong and continue to breathe, though in a broken breath pattern. Inhale, two short breaths and exhale, two short breaths. Accent the second inhale and exhale of each breath. Inhale, *inhale,* exhale, *exhale…*

4 Continue breathing for 10 full breaths. Maintain a pure and stable position, emphasising the need for firm, flat abdominals and depressing the shoulder blades. Before you lie down bend your knees toward your chest to protect the lower back.

NOTE

Realise the transition from the initial Breathing Exercise, to Chest Lift Holding and now to the Hundred. Learn to coordinate your diaphragm and deep abdominal muscles so that you develop a strong 'centre' and abdominal stamina. Throughout this process always endeavour to relax the muscles you don't need to use.

MODIFICATION

If you have a vulnerable neck and back, or if you lack strength, the Hundred is still suitable to practise with your head down (on a pillow if necessary) and your feet resting on a chair. This is an appropriate exercise as an extension to the Breathing Exercise, as you can develop core abdominal strength in a gentle manner.

Warm Up

(continued)

Roll Up (Prep & Full)

1 Start sitting with your legs comfortably bent in front of you and your hands at the back of your thighs. Lengthen your spine, lift your abdominal muscles inward and upward... and drop your shoulders. Breathe in.

2 As you exhale, pull your deep abdominals further toward your spine so that your pelvis can easily roll away from your thighs. Relax your thigh muscles (and use your arms if necessary) as you train your abdominals to articulate spinal movement.

3 Inhale, maintaining the round shape of your spine and strong centre.

4 As you exhale, rock forward toward your legs, keeping the spine and pelvis in exactly the same position. This resembles the top part of a typical 'sit up', so train your abdominals to stabilise your spine.

5 Repeat 3-5 times. Use your arms to assist the movement if your abdominals are struggling.

6 For the full Roll Up, roll your pelvis back from your thighs as you exhale and continue rolling through the back of your waist, then your ribcage and finally allow your head to touch the floor. Reach your arms overhead to stretch the shoulders and challenge your spinal stability.

7 Inhale, raising your arms to the ceiling. Draw the shoulders down, ribs down and shrink the waist.

8 Drop your chin gently and as you exhale roll forward, pressing the ribs into the floor, then press your abdominals very deeply toward your spine as you continue to roll forward to a sitting position.

9 Inhale, emphasise the drawing back of your abdominals and begin to roll your hip bones away from your thighs. Keep your shoulders relaxed.

10 Repeat 3-5 times. Continue to use your arms if you need assistance with a smooth rolling action. Straighten your legs as you become stronger to challenge pelvic stability and fluid spinal movement. Be conscious not to miss out on rolling through the lumbar spine.

NOTE
Remember how important symmetry is throughout the body. Ensure that you roll evenly through the spine – with left and right sides equal – and no jerky movements.

ABDOMINAL STRENGTHENING

Purpose *The essence of Pilates is strengthening the 'centre' – or 'powerhouse'. The following few exercises specifically require you to keep your pelvis anchored, abdominals flat, and control of your upper body and limb movement.*

SINGLE LEG STRETCH

1 Begin on your back with your legs in the tabletop position. Curl your head and chest forward as per the Hundred exercise, then reach your hands toward your ankles. Ensure your hips, back, ribcage and shoulders are stable and prepare your abdominals strongly. Breathe in.

2 As you exhale extend one leg directly away from you at a reasonable height and distance for you to maintain optimal low back stability. Emphasise scooping your abdominals.

3 Breathe in and return your leg to the tabletop position. Focus: shoulders down and stomach in.

4 Exhale, extending your other leg.

5 Inhale, draw the leg back in.

6 Continue to alternate leg extensions for 10-20 repetitions, though rest if you start to lose form.

OBLIQUE LIFTS

1 Begin on your back with your legs at the tabletop position and your hands behind your head. Ensure pelvis, spine, ribs and shoulders are all stable on the floor and that your elbows are both in your vision. Breathe in and prepare your abdominals.

2 As you exhale, drop your chin gently and roll your shoulders forward, leaning on one side of your ribcage more than the other. (Aim one shoulder to the opposite hip bone.) Don't rotate the body dramatically and keep your hips really still.

3 Inhale as you roll down. Take a brief moment to be stable and keep strong.

4 Exhale, curling up to the other side. Pelvis stable, stomach scooping, ribcage pressing into the floor, shoulder blades stable and flat, chin dropped and both elbows moving in the same direction as your shoulders.

5 Inhale, roll down.

6 Alternate sides, 6-10 repetitions. Maintain a moderate pace and control your breathing.

ABDOMINAL STRENGTHENING

(continued)

DOUBLE LEG STRETCH

1 Begin as for the Oblique Lifts, although with your hands placed on your knees. Breathe in, focusing on a strong 'centre.'

2 Exhale, dropping your chin gently and rolling your chest forward. Reach your arms down by your hips just off the floor. Extend both legs (appropriate to abdominal strength and pelvic/lumbar stability.)

3 As you inhale, raise your arms to the ceiling without compromising your position.

4 Exhale, circling your arms sideways so that they then reach back down by your hips. Emphasise your abdominals zipping and shoulder blades flattening.

5 Breathe in, bend your knees (first) and lie down, bring your legs to tabletop and your hands to your knees. Keep flattening your abdominals as you lie down, because this is essentially your preparation to roll straight back up again.

6 Repeat 5-10 repetitions.

NOTE
Coordinate abdominal strength, breathing, flowing movement and multi-directional manoeuvres.

MODIFICATION
While you are gaining abdominal strength and control over the choreography, keep your legs in the tabletop position, or place your feet on a chair or on the floor.

SPINAL MOVEMENT & CONTROL

Purpose *Joseph Pilates was quoted as saying that you're as young as your spine is flexible. Fluid, coordinated spinal articulation exercises in various forms help restore moveability to your spine.*

PELVIC CURL

1 Start in the preparatory position with your arms resting by your sides. Breathe in, feeling the breadth of your back on the floor and an awareness of the pelvic floor and deep abdominals.

2 As you exhale, press the abdominals in toward your spine, rolling your tailbone skyward. Continue to peel your pelvis, and gradually your spine, from the floor. Press both feet equally into the floor to ensure both hips remain symmetrical.

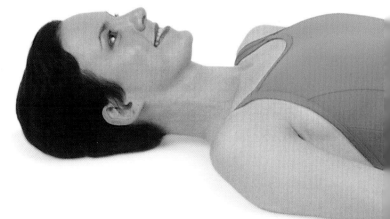

3 Take time to breathe in as you secure the high position. Relax your neck, shoulders and ribcage. Strengthen your ankles, thighs and hips.

4 Exhale, roll down starting from the shoulders. Articulate through the spine, roll through the back of your waist before the hips touch the floor.

5 Repeat 3-5 times.

PROGRESSION

To challenge the strength of your legs and back, and the stability of your pelvis, lift one foot off the floor while you are at the top of the curl. Do one leg lift each side, without straining the lower back or dropping one hip down, then roll back to the floor. Breathe calmly, one breath for each movement.

NOTE

While your abdominals secure your lower back, you lift your tail from the floor by means of the hamstring and lower fibres of the gluteal muscles. Imagine the muscles you sit on. Be aware to balance on your shoulder blades and not your neck at the top of the movement.

Spinal Movement & Control

(continued)

Spinal Mobility

1 Lie on your side with a pillow under your head. Bend your knees and reach your arms directly in front of your chest. Lengthen your spine and retract your shoulder blades gently.

2 As you inhale, raise your arm to the ceiling without rolling backward. Keep your shoulder blade flat and your neck relaxed.

3 Exhale, rolling your ribcage, shoulders and head backward while maintaining a long position with your outstretched arm and not allowing the shoulder to collapse toward your neck.

4 Inhale, stay. You should feel your upper back moving gently and feel associated stretches through the ribcage and chest. Try to keep your shoulder blade flattening down toward your waist.

5 As you exhale, raise your arm to the ceiling and return to your initial position.

6 Repeat 3-4 times each side.

SPINAL MOVEMENT & CONTROL

(continued)

SPINE STRETCH

1 Start sitting up straight with your legs stretched out in front of you, just wider than your hips. Bend your knees if you need to in order to achieve an ideal straight back posture. Lift your abdominal muscles and drop your shoulders. Inhale.

2 Exhale, nodding your chin down and slowly rolling your spine down toward the floor in front of you. Try to articulate through each level of your spine to encourage better joint movement throughout. Round 'forward' as far as you are comfortable without slouching back into your pelvis or rolling too far forward off your sitting bones.

3 Breathe in. Relax your shoulders and expand through the back of your ribcage to breathe. Keep the pelvic floor and abdominals lifted.

4 As you exhale, emphasise your abdominals lifting up away from the floor and begin rolling your lower back up to neutral. Gradually rebuild your spine to an upright position, relaxing your shoulders as you sit up completely.

5 Repeat 3-5 times, with an option of remaining in the stretch forward position for two or three full breaths before rolling up. Flexing the ankles at the bottom of the movement will intensify the stretch.

SIDE STABILITY

Purpose *While balancing on the smaller surface area of your thigh, ribcage and shoulder, your 'core stabiliser' and hip muscles have to work harder, while you develop the coordination of added leg movement.*

SIDE LEG LIFTS

1 Lie on your side with both legs straight. (You may need a pillow under your head.) Elongate your spine, keep your abdominals and ribs drawn in and try to make sure that your hip bones are vertically aligned so that your spine is not rotating.

2 Breathe in, lifting your top leg slightly. Don't move your pelvis, lift through your waist muscles and keep both knees straight and pointing forward.

3 As you exhale, lift your underneath leg to join your top leg and lower them both together. Throughout this transition, your pelvis and spine should not move. Press your abdominals in toward your spine especially in preparation to lift the second leg. (Be conscious not to allow the legs to swing behind you.)

4 Repeat 8-10 times, then…

SIDE STABILITY

(continued)

SIDE LEG LIFTS *(continued)*

5 Keep your legs together and hover them just off the floor. Emphasise a long, strong waist, maintaining a sensation of a connection between your ribs and hip bones. Lift and lower just your top leg, exhaling every time you draw the legs together. Keep the underneath leg still and reaching out long.

6 Repeat 5-10 times.

7 Then, lower and lift your underneath leg, exhaling as you lift it each time. Maintain abdominals and keep an even pace. Keep your top leg still and lengthened.

8 Repeat 5-10 times.

9 Repeat ALL on the other side.

SIDE STABILITY

(continued)

SIDE KICK

1 Lie on your side with your underneath leg bent and forward at a right angle. Stretch your top leg directly below you, straight and slightly above hip level. Ensure that your torso is aligned so that your spine does not rotate.

2 As you inhale, flex your ankle and take your top leg forward with a double pulse, only as far as you can maintain an ideal spinal alignment. Keep your knee pointing forward and your leg slightly above hip level.

3 Exhale, point your foot, sweeping your leg straight back without disturbing the position of your pelvis and spine.

4 Repeat 8-10 times, then on the other side.

Scapula Stability & Back Strengthening

Purpose *Shoulder, upper back, abdominal and hip muscles need strength for good posture. The following exercises challenge their endurance in a less stable position.*

4 Point Kneeling Swimming

1 Start kneeling on your hands and knees, with your knees under hip joints and hands under shoulder joints. Your spine and head should be in neutral alignment. Engage the deep abdominal and pelvic floor muscles and stabilise your shoulder blades.

2 As you breathe in, slide your opposite hand and foot along the floor and lift them slightly. Try to keep your body still and stable.

3 Exhale, drawing them back to the 4-point position.

4 Repeat with the opposite sides, and continue alternating for 8-10 repetitions.

NOTE
Having to support some of your body weight with your arms and shoulders forces you to think about the position of your shoulder blades and upper sections of your spine. Try to develop the muscles around your shoulder blades for upper trunk strength and continue to reinforce the abdominal and hip muscles for greater pelvic and lower back stability. Keep your head lifted slightly and your chin gently tucked.

GLUTE PULSES

1 Begin kneeling on your hands and knees. Lift through your abdominals and stabilise your shoulders. In a mirror, check the side view, that your spine appears to be quite level as a 'tabletop' is.

2 Lift one leg backward, and, keeping it bent, pulse with small lifts toward the ceiling. Only lift as far as your spine does not change shape. Exhale with each up movement and ensure that the movement happens from the hip joint and not the knee.

3 Repeat 10-20 pulses on each leg.

NOTE
Ensure shoulders are drawn down, abdominals lift up, hips remain square and your head does not drop too low. Think of lifting your thigh each pulse with the muscles you 'sit on'.

Scapula Stability & Back Strengthening

(continued)

PLANK PREP

1 Still in your 4-point kneeling position, place the heels of your hands forward where the tips of your fingers were, and lean on your hands in this new position, keeping the knees where they were. Tuck your toes under... stabilise your shoulders... lift your abdominals... and engage your glutes – mildly tucking your tail under.

2 Breathe in, straightening one leg so that you are a straight line from heel to shoulder on that side.

3 Exhale, straighten your other leg so that you are now in a 'plank', or 'push up', position. Emphasise shoulders down, stomach up and your 'seat' muscles very slightly squeezing under. Stretch your leg muscles long.

4 Inhale, bend your first knee to kneel again.

5 Exhale, bend the other knee. Your torso should remain fairly still in space regardless of where your legs are moving.

6 Repeat 4-6 times, alternating which leg starts first each time.

7 Repeat 2-4 times, where both legs stretch or bend together – exhaling upon any movement.

Scapula Stability & Back Strengthening

(continued)

Back Extension with Arms

1 Lie face down, resting your forehead on a rolled towel. Place your arms at 90 degree angles next to your shoulders. Realise where your anchor points are on the floor – your ribcage and your pelvic bones. (You may require a folded towel, or small pillow, under your abdomen to support the lumbar spine.) Draw your abdominal muscles up like a zip action without moving your spine. Inhale.

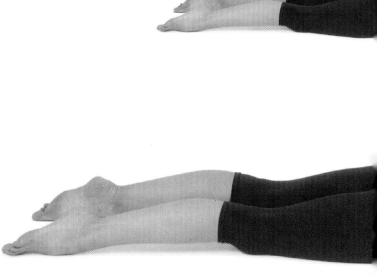

2 As you exhale, mildly draw your shoulders away from your ears and hover your forehead and chest just off the floor, while you anchor your lower ribcage to the floor.

3 Breathe in, maintaining your shoulder posture, and lift your hands. Keep a strong connection with your abdominals and keep the pubic bone on the floor.

4 Exhale, lower your hands without going 'round' shouldered.

5 Inhale, relax your body down.

6 Repeat 3-6 times.

PROGRESSION

If you have good shoulder movement and a stable lower back, lift your chest, keeping your shoulder blades drawn flat... then lift your hands, then your elbows. Then, elbows down to the floor first, hands down, then chest down. Breathe through the movement... maintain strong abdominals... balance on your ribs... shoulder blades stable and flat... neck tension free... chin tucked mildly and whenever your elbows lift, ensure that your shoulders don't drop and become rounded.

MODIFICATION

If you find it too difficult to lift your hands, it is probably because you are allowing your shoulders to stay 'rounded' forward. Omit the arm movement and focus on strengthening your upper back without neck strain. Visualise bending backward from the upper thoracic area, much like the image of the Egyptian sphinx. Don't look up – keep your chin slightly down as you lift your chest.

Scapula Stability & Back Strengthening

(continued)

Caterpillar

1 Kneel on your hands and knees, as for Swimming and Glute Pulses. Inhale.

2 As you exhale, draw your abdominal muscles up and tuck your tail under, curving your lower back. Continue to gradually curl your spine into a round shape allowing your head to drop down at the last.

3 Inhale, expanding your ribs.

4 Exhale, lift your tail bone skyward slightly to allow your lower back to flatten and gradually undulate the spine through to a neutral and mildly extended position, ending with drawing your shoulders down and looking up slightly. Keep your stomach and pelvic floor muscles lifted.

5 Inhale.

6 Repeat 3-4 times in full.

PELVIC STABILITY & HIP ENDURANCE

Purpose *The ability to move your hip joints without moving your pelvis or lower back will help you achieve greater hip joint mobility, as well as tone the hip and thigh muscles.*

CUSHION SQUEEZE

1 Start in the preparatory position on your back. Place a cushion between your knees and keep your feet no wider than the width of your sitting bones. Breathe evenly and focus on your abdominals. Inhale.

2 Exhale, squeezing your thighs together without moving your pelvis. Elongate your breaths, so it takes about 4 counts to squeeze.

3 As you inhale, take about 4 counts to release your knees. Maintain your pelvic floor and deep abdominals.

4 Repeat 4-5 times, then again with your legs in the tabletop position, ensuring greater stability throughout the spine and pelvis.

CLAM

1 Lie on your side with your knees bent and your feet in line with your tail. Don't allow your 'top' hip to roll forward: ensure pelvic alignment and light abdominal bracing. You may require a pillow for your head. Inhale.

2 Exhale, keeping your heels relaxed together, lift your top knee in an arc motion without moving your pelvis at all.

3 Inhale as you slowly lower your leg.

4 Repeat 10-15 times for each leg. Keep a moderate pace to achieve greater hip control and endurance.

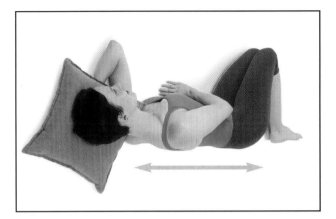

FULL BODY INTEGRATION

Purpose *Ultimately, Pilates exercises are aimed at you being able to integrate all the principles into sequenced movement and mobilise some parts of the body while stabilising the pelvis and shoulder girdle. Teaser and various preparations will challenge your coordination, balance, strength and control.*

TEASER PREP

1 Start on your back with your knees bent. Reach your arms overhead and ensure that your abdominals are braced, that your ribs are flat on the floor and that your shoulders are drawing down.

2 As you breathe in reach both arms to the ceiling and deepen the bracing action of your abdominals.

3 Exhale as you nod your chin and roll your spine off the floor until you are balancing on the back of your pelvis. Reach your arms forward and keep your legs still.

4 Breathe in as you lengthen your torso on a slight incline away from your thighs. Imagine your tail as an anchor on the floor. Lift and press your abdominals firmly to your spine and raise your arms to challenge your strength.

5 Exhale. Emphasise rolling through your lower back. Control the spinal articulation back to the floor and finish reaching both arms overhead. Repeat 3-5 times, aiming for optimal movement control and flow.

STRETCHES

Purpose *The following stretches target some key areas that are generally prone to tightness. Take care to stretch within your range of comfort. Improving or maintaining your suppleness is just as important as muscle strengthening.*

HIP FLEXOR, PSOAS & HAMSTRING STRETCH

1 Begin kneeling on one knee with your other leg bent in front of you. Legs should be parallel, with the majority of your body weight on your back knee. Tuck your tail under and transfer your weight onto your front foot slightly...in order to facilitate a stretch at the front of your (kneeling) hip. Don't allow your lower back to arch or your hips to twist to the side. Breathe through the stretch.

2 Lunge forward and place your hands either side of your front foot. Take your body weight onto your hands, the front thigh and foot. Allow your back leg to relax so that the front of the hip stretches. Continue to breathe.

3 Take your full body weight onto the front foot and stand on the back foot, straightening both legs, keeping one forward and one back (depending on your flexibility). Both feet should point forward and your priority is keeping your hips square. You can bend one or both knees slightly to achieve the hamstring stretch with good pelvic alignment. Relax your head, neck and shoulders. Breathe.

4 Repeat all stretches on the other side, holding each one for between 30-90 seconds.

STRETCHES

(continued)

ADDUCTOR STRETCH & FROG

1 Sit on the floor and extend one leg out to the side, as far as you can keeping both hip bones square to the front. Keep your other leg bent in front of you. Lean forward carefully and take your body weight onto your arms if you can. Depending on your hip joint range and flexibility, you may be more comfortable on a couple of phone books or even on the edge of a bench/ table. Ensure the knee of your outstretched leg points up to the ceiling. Breathe.

2 Repeat on the other leg.

3 Still sitting, bring the soles of your feet together and allow your knees to open out to the sides. Depending on your hip range you may feel this stretch in the inner or outer hip/thigh. Breathe.

STRETCHES

(continued)

MERMAID

1 Sitting cross-legged on the floor (if comfortable, otherwise sit on the edge of a bench/table with your legs together) lengthen your spine and raise one arm, leaving your other hand near the floor close to your knee.

2 Carefully bend sideways towards the low arm for a side stretch on the opposite side. Use your abdominal muscles and allow your head and neck to relax as you lean on your bottom arm. Breathe, and when returning to a straight spine, engage the abdominals and slowly return as you exhale.

3 Repeat 1-3 times each side. You may alternate.

MODIFICATION
You may need something higher to lean on if it is difficult to stretch this far. Be cautious of this stretch if you have lower back pain.

GLOSSARY

ABDOMINALS
Common term for the group of abdominal muscles. The 'six-pack' crunches you forward, the obliques (waist muscles) rotate and twist your trunk, and the deep layer of abdominal muscle (transversus abdominus) works to stabilise your spine against any of the actions just noted.

ADDUCTORS
Muscles of the inner thighs, which draw one leg toward the other.

GLUTES
The gluteal group of muscles are those of the buttocks, which contribute to hip movement and stability of the pelvis and lower back.

HAMSTRINGS
The group of muscles at the back of the thigh running from the sitting bone to the back of the knee joint. These assist in backward leg motion and bending of the knee.

HIP FLEXORS
Muscles of the front of the hip (groin area), one of which is the psoas. They act to lift the thigh toward the torso.

LUMBAR SPINE
The five vertebrae that form the lower back region, above the pelvis.

PELVIC FLOOR
A thin layering of muscles suspended across the pelvic girdle. It supports the weight of the abdominal organs and shares nerve connection with the respiratory diaphragm and deep abdominal muscles. Activation of the pelvic floor therefore assists in stabilising the lower back and contributes to the strengthening of the deep abdominal muscles. This is important for improving your posture.

SCAPULA
The shoulder blade, which helps make up the shoulder joint and provides attachments for most of the muscles of the upper back. Stabilising the scapulae so that they are flat against the back of the ribcage is essential for good posture.

THORACIC SPINE
The twelve vertebrae that form the upper and middle back. These vertebrae also provide attachment sites for the ribs. (Note: the cervical spine is that of the neck; the sacrum and coccyx make up the most lower part of the spine).

CONCLUSION

When you practise Pilates with purpose and consistency, you will achieve freedom of movement, improved sense of centre and balance, and greater levels of energy. The aim is to provide you with a flexible, more supple body. With regular practice, improvements in your physical ability will also become apparent. Remember that your goal is to coordinate your breathing, correct abdominal bracing, pelvic and lumbar stability and the release of unnecessary strain.

Mastering the 'choreography' of the exercises is of course necessary for the development of all the Pilates principles. However this must remain a secondary objective - 'quality over quantity' is what you require. Focus your mind, keep a moderate pace and keep reminding yourself of the principles behind the movement. This will allow you to gain the most benefit from *More Simply Pilates*.

More Simply Pilates is an all rounded home workout program designed for you to enhance your fitness regime. For greater benefit from your practise of Pilates, or if you require assistance with your comprehension of this unique exercise philosophy, visit a reputable Pilates studio.

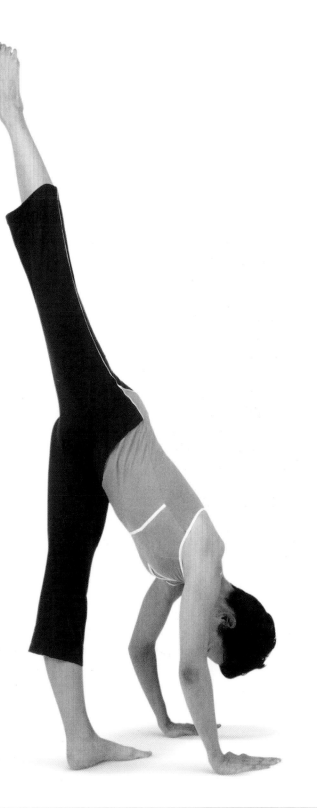

ABOUT THE AUTHOR

JENNIFER POHLMAN was first introduced to Pilates as a dance student whilst completing a Bachelor of Dance degree at the Victorian College of the Arts in Melbourne. She later trained as an instructor and taught the Pilates Method in Brisbane and Gold Coast studios before establishing her own Gold Coast studio at Kirra, called 'Pilates InsideOut'.